I saw a
DINOSAUR

by Mary Atkinson

make
believe
ideas

Get the most from this reader

Before reading:

- Look at the pictures and discuss them together. Ask questions such as, "Is this dinosaur big or small?"

- Relate the topic to your child's world. For example, say: "Which of your toy dinosaurs looks like this one?"

- Familiarise your child with book vocabulary by using terms such as *word*, *letter*, *title*, *author* and *text*.

During reading:

- Prompt your child to sound out unknown words. Draw attention to neglected middle or end sounds.

- Encourage your child to use the pictures as clues to unknown words.

- Occasionally, ask what might happen next, and then check together as you read on.

This book belongs to

. . . .

Photographs courtesy of Shutterstock unless noted as follows:
Make Believe Ideas: 14-15 (dinosaur).

Dinosaur model on pp. 14-15 supplied by:
www.dinosaurtime.co.uk

- Monitor your child's understanding. Repeated readings can improve fluency and comprehension.

- Keep reading sessions short and enjoyable. Stop if your child becomes tired or frustrated.

• •

After reading:

- Discuss the book. Encourage your child to form opinions with questions such as, "What did you like best about this book?"

- Help your child work through the fun activities at the back of the book. Then ask him or her to reread the story. Praise any improvement.

I went back in time to see some dinosaurs.

I saw a dinosaur with pointy plates. I took a photo.

17

I saw a dinosaur with big teeth. I **did not** take a photo!

Discussion Questions

1. What did the explorer do each time she saw a dinosaur?

2. Why didn't she take a photo of the last dinosaur?

3. Would you like to take photos of dinosaurs? Why?

❧ Sight Words ❧

Learning sight words helps you read fluently. Practise these sight words from the book. Use them in sentences of your own.

I

with

a

saw

see

not

went

took

೨ Rhyming Words ೨

Can you find the rhyming pairs?
Say them aloud.

big

saw

took

dig

paw

book

Writing Practice

Read the words, and then trace them with your finger.

some

with

take

plate

photo

teeth

🦕 Silly Sentences 🦕

Have fun filling in the gap in each sentence. Use the ideas below or make up your own.

I saw a dinosaur with ....

I saw a ....
I took a photo.